ACID REFLUX:

HOW TO STOMACH THIS ECONOMY

Written by

Dr. Tori Brown

Published by **Success Lockdown Group LLC**

Acid Reflux: How To Stomach This Economy Copyright © 2020 by **Dr. Tori Brown**

All rights reserved. Printed in The United States of America. No part of this publication may be reproduced, stored in a retrieval system or transmitted in any form or by any means electronic, mechanical, photography, copying, recording or otherwise, without prior written permission of the publisher, except in the case of brief quotations embodied in critical articles and reviews. The author rights to "freedom speech' protected by and with the 1st Amendment of the constitution of the United States of America. Books may be purchased for educational, business, or sales promotional use. For information please email successlockdown@gmail.com.

Published in the United States by Success Lockdown Group LLC

Located in Tampa Florida

ISBN: 978-0-578-69890-8 (Print)

ISBN: 978-1-7351332-0-1 (E Book)

Library of Congress Control Number: 2020939188

First Edition

DEDICATION

I dedicate this to my Most Valuable Player (MVP) - Momma. Thank you for believing in me when all of them closed their eyes so they could not see my tears and while some went to deaf ears so they wouldn't hear me crying. Every time they knocked me down. You just built me back up. Now I can pick up the next person and build them up. We got this!

TABLE OF CONTENTS

Dedication 3
Foreword 5
Introduction 11
Chapter 1 The Have & The Have Nots 16
Chapter 2 Acid Reflux 22
Chapter 3 Time for a Check-Up 30
Chapter 4 Dr.'s Orders 39
Chapter 5 Building an Ark 45
Understanding & Addressing Your Credit Report ... 58
Acknowledgements 65
Author 68

FOREWORD

Written by Jah'tia Haynes

The American Dream is not free; it is sold separately.

No, that is not exactly how the saying goes. The original saying goes on to talk about the hustle, which is essentially the same thing. Both of which are lies. You do not have to work hard for what you get in life and there is no American Dream -- at least not how it has been marketed. Yes, I said marketed. That is because the saying has become more of a promotional message than a reality for most. In fact, I read somewhere that The American Dream started as a marketing campaign by Fannie Mae. Another source said it was coined in the 1900s by James Truslow Adams in his book The Epic of America. No matter how you define the dream, most of us are currently going through a mind-altering experience where the veil has been lifted. We realize the fairytale that we have been sold all our lives was simply an entertaining story of a life that was only accessible to some. In today's reality, cities are locked down, schools are closed, banks are failing, and major corporations are gone along with our jobs. This feels like a nightmare. But that is only if you choose not to wake up.

Dr. Tori Brown has been working to prepare individuals, families, and communities for the upcoming shift of wealth for quite some time. In fact, that is what brought us together -- aside from being related and getting to know each other much later in our journeys. Her mission is to build entrepreneurs and expose them to opportunities through funding. My mission is to build entrepreneurs and expose them to opportunities through marketing and public relations. Our journeys are so different and yet our missions are so similar. We knew the shift was going to happen, we just did not expect it to hit like this. We both have faced different obstacles that exposed us to the reality of the American Dream. She shares a few of her obstacles in this book, which I found helpful in decoding my own life through our everyday conversations.

An experience I can recall is when I learned I had been accepted in to one of the most prestigious universities in America on a full-ride scholarship for first-generation college students. Yes, University of Florida, home of the innovative Gator Nation. Then came my next decision, what to major in. Once again, I began weighing what would guarantee my stability in life against what would make me happy. I chose stability and decided to begin my freshman year in college on pre-dental track. What? That was so far from any of my creative passions. But it was safe, or so I thought. Did you know that orthodontists are deemed non-essential during this pandemic? Writing this made me realize how much foresight God had on my future. Nonetheless, I constantly struggled with wondering if I made the right decision. And then it hit me -- I was not completely fulfilled on a pre-dental track and I hated science.

During this time, I had already been involved in a few organizations of which I designed flyers for various events on campus, so I decided to switch my major to advertising. After switching majors and sitting through a semester or two, I realized that I once again was not fulfilled. Though I like to design and ads, I felt that it was too restricting, and I wanted more flexibility in my career. So, I went on a search to find my path. I did not expect to find a mentor and that was exactly what the doctor prescribed. She was majoring in Public Relations and was gracious enough to take me under her wings. She taught me new things and introduced me into situations that forced me to grow. Through this major, my first reporting class would turn my blog assignment into an internship with Fresh Docs Inc. From there I became part of the DocTori2.0 business development team with the mission to fight gentrification with participation.

If I can be completely real, college was a series of wins and losses, life experiences and acid reflux. I made some great decisions. I made some not so great decisions. What I realized is that I did not love school or at least the way it was currently being administered. I was in love with the quest for knowledge and bringing it back to the people. The truth is that it does not matter where or how you access information whether that be in a classroom or from your couch. The key is to keep learning no matter where you are and apply that knowledge everywhere you are. After college, I landed two jobs: my dream job that did not pay much and a job working at a big-time financial firm that would be my first introduction into big business and the real world. It was there I got a glimpse into just how big the corporate world was and how small of a piece of the pie you get as an employee. No matter how hard you worked, saved, or how much money you made the company...that paycheck was still the same every two weeks. I could barely afford my overpriced apartment; car payment and insurance and I was still in debt from school. I was eventually fired. The American dream was not a dream at all -- it was a nightmare. Acid Reflux kicked in. But it was just the push I needed to run my business full-time.

Dr. Tori and I reconnected at just the right time. I had transitioned into entrepreneurship full-time. We were catching up on life, business, health and of course finances. During our life-changing conversations, she connected my acid reflux to stress and everything else I was experiencing in my life -- including my finances. It was here that she stressed the importance of funding your future. She put me on the program and began getting my finances together. What do the words "reflux," "American," and "information" have in common? They both have the letter "I" or "U" in them because that is where the American dream begins. Despite your obstacles or ailments, with access to the proper information, you can live your own dream. Information is powerful because it is the only thing that is constant and ever evolving at the same time. Throughout my entire life, I have been on a quest for information. It was not about the institution or the teacher but the transfer of knowledge. This is the most valuable asset in our economy. It is how teachers, lawyers and doctors make money. It has nothing to do with a degree. They are paid to access information that others did not have so that they could charge for it later down the road.

When you go to college you are not paying for a degree. It's virtually useless in today's economy and it really depends on your career path. If you do not believe me, take a look around at all of your educated friends and family who were not working in their respective fields or were barely making enough to make ends meet prior to the pandemic. I bet you know plumbers and leading managers who make more than some graduates. This is the shocking truth and reality of the American Dream. You are paying for access to information and that information does not always come from your teachers. Sometimes, it comes from your peers, mentors, conversations, and experiences. But that is the beauty of it. You do not have to go to college to access information or people. There is always an abundance of information and teachers at our disposal. Dr. Tori went through the struggles and losses in business, so you would not have to. She is going to teach you everything you need to stomach this economy. You are already here; you just have to lock-in on the information.

INTRODUCTION

2020 Changed Everything

On March 10th, 2020 one of the most talented producers in the music industry was in my office creating beats. The corporate offices of Tampa, Florida have never heard such creativity and skill as we laughed about music, business, and real estate. Why real estate? Why not? We had just had a conversation about the properties he acquired in Miami. He secured property and under his suggestion, I had just acquired property too. Not just any property but waterfront property with the view of beautiful Miami. That's what the plans had been over the last 6 months of planning to secure a Florida portfolio of real estate properties.

Having been instrumental in helping clients access business funding for real estate portfolio projects over the years, I was now starting to work on building my own in Florida. What was next for me and my business development team? That's right the next step was to increase the amount of real estate investors in key cities throughout the country to build real estate projects. These projects would create affordable luxury living for everyday working people. The plan was in motion and everything was set. We had move-in dates for the Miami properties and furniture was set to deliver in early April. By the time Friday, March 13th, 2020 hit, I was starting to get another cold it seems. Cold chills, some fever, runny nose, and a cough was causing me to only want to lay down and sleep.

On March 13th, 2020 my mother told me about a deadly disease that was sweeping across cities and killing people. She said they projected it to be worse than the flu. As I laid in bed there was this temptation to Google the market and from there, I could see stocks that were once $30 a share or more were trickling down the $7 or $8 a share. I'm like, what is really going on? So, I began to read different things that were going on in the market. Who was injecting funding into what companies for a race to find the vaccination for this deadly virus? The news was on 24/7 as my mother gave me updates on different states that were reporting the number of people going into the hospital and dying. How could this be and what was happening? I knew from years of research that the economy will reset itself every 8 to 10 years by going into a recession.

I was prepared for the recession though. My credit scores were almost 800 FICO. My family and business partners all had over 700 personal credit scores. My business development team had already started building real estate investment group systems that would help working-class employees become real estate investors. In fact, for many years this has been the track and purpose of setting up my company. I often felt like Noah building an Ark for rain that has not yet hit. According to the bible, the people had never seen rain before, so they didn't know what to fully expect. That's how it is when you are building an Ark. Here I am for the past 2 years, -- I was building a company that would serve as a business development incubator system that would help people improve their credit, start their own business, and then get their business funded to create funds for real estate investment projects.

These projects would allow everyday people to fight gentrification with participation. It had become very obvious that the people who were most angered by community gentrification were mostly the ones who were disadvantaged and could not participate in purchasing their own commercial and residential properties in their own communities. This is something to become very frustrated about. It's a slap in the face to work hard every day on a job 8 to 10 hours sometimes and still come home to a place that doesn't have the best plumbing. It's a frustrating period when you want to do better and for whatever reason, you cannot find the avenue to doing better. What pain to feel when the house you're forced to live in is owned by a landlord that refuses to fix the toilet or has not bothered to even plant new grass on an eroding yard that your children have to play in. Even worse, how can your children play when the neighborhood is full of crime and you have the fear of being robbed or killed?

This, of course, is not every neighborhood that faces gentrification but it's a close realistic glimpse on how things are experienced in some low-income environments. What is the solution? There can be many solutions and there can also be none that apply to every population. The one thing that could be agreed on is trying something is better than doing nothing. What results do you get out of nothing? NOTHING! With so many things going on in this country, we have to be willing to make changes and make them fast. There are so many things to consider as options to surviving during this national pandemic. The *haves* and the *have nots* are definitely two different types of populations. The difference between the have and the have nots is the information one has access to while the other one does not. You must make a decision as to which one you are. For there is a distinction and a direction in which both can take which will result in self-sustainability during this economic downfall.

When you see big companies stealing money earmarked for small businesses you recognize and know that corporate greed has taken its overindulgence of pie. Where is the small business owner's piece of the pie? How about the small business owners who were cut out of the inheritance of the benefit that comes with being a small business owner? Where does that leave new businesses to survive and new business owners that want to get started? It can leave them afraid and alone. Too scared to leave the house to work 9 to 5, but just as scared to stay home and build a business with the cut-throat imagery of what being a business looks like. It can be done with the right tools and faith of Noah. Building on blind faith and trust that God is a provider and He will always show His provisions in the land. Just build. While you build, I can show you How to Stomach This Economy.

Chapter 1

The Have & The Have Nots

Tyler Perry is just pure genius. To take his talent from sleeping in a car to a multi-million-dollar platform of Television Production and Filmmaking. It seems he replaced his pain with his passion. One of the hit series he produced is called The Have & The Have Nots. It's an amazing concept show that shows the interaction of those who are rich and those who are struggling. No matter what the financial positions of the characters are, none of them seem to be exempt from the struggles, hurt, and family drama.

I just love the character Candice Young all while I'm hating her. This actress does such a great job in this character that it makes me wonder what she is up to, even when she is playing another character in a movie. I was waiting any minute for Tika Sumpter, who she played as the character in Sonic The Hedge Hodge, to turn into a villain and expose Sonic at any moment in the movie. That's what great acting and an even greater production does as we in the audience react to what is seen. We do this every day and most likely even more as the news is on in almost every household. News is designed to inform. It is also created to get a reaction. I admit that during this whole 2020 introduction to the

Virus Pandemic, my reactions were just like some of yours. I'm scared most days. I'm frustrated with a feeling of house arrest other days. I'm cursing at the television set just like you are -- every day.

Our reaction to what we see is our reaction. It's just a human response to the daily routine of being uncertain. What we are uncertain about is put in our face day after day. Everything closing down because of the threat of the death tolls we are seeing every day in the media. This put millions of people out of work all over the country. Even if you perceived that a recession was coming you did not have the ability to project that it was going to come like this...by deadly force. The processing of failed unemployment claims through a non-functioning website was just one issue. On the other hand, the other issue is applying for relief money in the midst of large corporations stealing money from these small businesses. The absolute shame should have been in how they were allowed to do it. Even more pressing, why were they allowed to do it?

This is a case of the haves vs. the have not. Remember the difference between the two is the information each has access to. One group has information and an "In" therefore their application was accepted, processed, and paid. No problem. Group two did not have the information so they were not privy to the process or protocol of applying. It can be quite disgusting how the "in" game gets played when it comes to entrepreneurship. It was always supposed to be the

"American Way" of business. This is kind of like the white picket fence dream we all were fed as a child. The American Dream that not all people get to see. Especially poor or low-income people. Where are their American Dreams?

Do all populations get to dream equally in America? Not where I am from. Living just a few miles away from Flint, Michigan growing up, who would have thought that their drinking water would taste so much different than ours in Saginaw, Michigan? Here we are surrounded by the Great Lakes of Michigan and to think that we live in a state where clean water is not available! Even when the Flint Water Crisis hit the newsfeed back in 2016; it sounded absurd that the America we live in located within the Great Lakes had a city that was drinking water for years that was slowly killing them. Not only was it killing their bodies, but it was killing their economy and it damn sure was killing their dreams. Was this a black or white thing? Or was it a poor or rich thing? We know that historically when people are low income and do not have the resources to make decisions for themselves, people with more power and structure will make it for them.

Where were the protesters that stood for the people of Flint the minute brown water started dripping out of their pipes? Where were the church leaders that stood up and said to their thousands of congregations of voters, we are not taking this shit anymore? Who spoke for the people the minute the water became brown?

Even worst, who would drink brown water every day and let others continue to believe that it was okay? Innocent and helpless people would. And that is what happened and continues to happen because people are not speaking up and speaking against humanity. Drinking clean water is a basic requirement especially for taxpayers and people that pay for their water in that community. Do you want to know what else is a basic requirement that should speak to humanity? Information. In its existence, information is necessary and when in the right hands, it can be used to either empower or isolate.

Give group one, The Haves described earlier, have information and they know what to do with it to move forward, and they do just that. This gives them access to things like money, great credit, real estate property, and power. They still have the same issues as the characters in the Tyler Perry Hit television show The Have and The Have Nots: family drama, pain, loss, stress etc. But, with financial resources in place, they can navigate through it just a little different than others. On the other hand, give group two the same information. If they are self-starting, faithful, and motivated just as so many have nots are, they can reach the same amount of success as the haves and even more so. The Have Nots do not have to continue to "have not" is my point. You do not have to stay in the rat race of not having.

If you are self-starting, if you are faithful, if you are motivated, you can change the face of your circumstances financially. I believe that once you change your mind, you can change your pockets. Do not be comfortable living your life as a have not. It's not cute, it's not "struggle valor," it's just "struggle" with no context as to why you are doing it. Sometimes we meet people in your lives and day in and day out we rock with them in the trenches of life. Maybe you lost a job and they lost a job and you both can't find a job and every day you both trade jobless stories. You build a relationship and conversational context with those that you can identify with and they can identify with you.

Both of you get caught up in what we call "struggle love" and you stay stuck. But as long as you got each other, that is what matters right? I don't think so. The have nots can get on a conversation together and exchange "broke stories" and never have a solution to get out of the struggle or the conversation about the struggle. "Struggle love" does not put food on the table. Information does. That's right! Information puts food on your table. Follow-through puts food on the table. Good credit takes ideas to market and sales to business bank accounts. Watch who you are talking to and what you are talking about. Be mindful of your conversations and your goals. You can do it. I promise you if you change your mind you will literally change your pockets.

Have your mind made up when it comes to refusing to be a "have not." Say it! "I will not have lack in my life anymore." Say it like you mean it and activate it. That's right activate the faith that you are Noah and you must build an ark. That ark is your protection from what we are facing in this economy. Be strong and courageous and keep your mouth off what I call, "poor talk." Don't do it. Read about the haves. Try to study the haves' behaviors as it relates to business, finances, and credit. Remember the true difference between the have and the have nots is the information you have access to.

Chapter 2

Acid Reflux

What is acid reflux? According to healthline.com, Acid reflux happens when contents from your stomach move up into your esophagus. It is also called acid regurgitation or gastroesophageal reflux. Mayoclinic.org says that Acid reflux occurs when the sphincter muscle at the lower end of your esophagus relaxes at the wrong time, allowing stomach acid to back up into your esophagus. This can cause heartburn and other signs and symptoms. Frequent or constant reflux can lead to what the medical professionals call gastroesophageal reflux disease (GERD).

Watching television on Thursday, April 16th, 2020 was beginning to feel just like acid reflux. If you have never had an occurrence of Acid Reflux in your life let me tell you how it feels. You are sick to your stomach and with a fullness as if you overate. The burning sensation on your stomach can cause your belly to feel like it is in serious knots. It is a burning kind of like feeling that you may not always be able to describe to others. Imagine everything you ate that day just stuck in one area of your stomach causing an acid feeling to send a blazing jolt up through your esophagus and into your throat. You clear your throat constantly because you feel like you have to cough.

Your chest can feel as if phlegm needs to be coughed up so you can spit it out. It often gives you the feeling that you're about to get a chest cold or pneumonia. The heartburn from it is very uncomfortable and the acid often slides upward leaving a slight tickle in your throat. You can soon begin to feel as if you are about to vomit liquid and the acid taste reaches your month as you swallow it back down. The nasty taste it leaves in your mouth is just as scorching as the liquid acid that feels like fire drips back in your throat as you swallow it back down. If you're used to it, you learn how to spit the taste back up. This can also happen while you are sleeping.

Imagine being woken up out of your sleep suddenly because it feels like a flame just went up your throat splashing into your nostrils as you gag and swallow. This can occur several times a night and if not properly treated can occur three or four times or more a week depending on what you ate. Acid reflux is both dangerous and painful. The minute you describe the feeling to a medical doctor they call it by name. GERD, gastroesophageal reflux disease. According to the National Institute of Diabetes and Digestive and Kidney Diseases (NIDDK), GERD affects about 20 percent of people in the United States. If left untreated, it can sometimes cause serious complications.

Let us go to Thursday, April 16th, 2020 and why on that date it was beginning to feel like acid reflux. News channels everywhere were making the same announcement. Money that was being set aside for the small businesses in this country was gone. How did this happen? And who were the actual funded business owners that I personally knew? Being in this field of business development, I know a lot of hardworking business owners; some with brick and mortar locations and others with home businesses. Nevertheless, they were qualified by the registered state as a small business. The headlines also began to speak about the multi-million-dollar businesses and billion-dollar businesses that were classified as small businesses that had taken all of the dough from the small bakers.

Who are the small bakers? The small bakers are people like single mothers that were juggling between homeschooling their kids and daily business operations while trying to stay safe at home. Another group of small bakers are the people who pay monthly for an office or building but could not go to these locations because of the virus. That's the fear of going to your office because we were told to stay at home because it was safer. And for that, I believe that staying at home is safer during the pandemic. However, this does not help the millions of small business owners that are incurring expenses daily, yet they see that their income has come to a complete stop. So out of distress, millions of business owners are informed to apply for funding to save their businesses. Yet the playing field for the application process is not even.

The business funding relief game had so many loopholes in it that several groups were not qualified properly for funds. People applied to banks as directed, but the banks had their selection of who could apply and who could not apply. The situation was just plain messy and unorganized. I remember reaching out to my bank on April 3rd, 2020 to submit my application for business support. The bankers did not have any information about where I would submit my application. They came to the conclusion that I should hold on to it until April 10th, 2020 because I would apply with that particular group of applicants.

April 10th, 2020 my business reached out to the bank again and they told us to hold the application because they were not finished setting up their website portal so that we could submit the application. We were told that the website portal would be ready on April 13th, 2020. As directed, we went to the site to see there were no portals in place to upload the application. We spoke to the banker again and they revealed that the site is not yet ready, and they would email me when it would be ready and available to accept applications. At this point, we went to another business bank to see if they had information to upload the application. Yes!!! Bingo they did. They had an upload login account where you could upload your application and attachment documents to apply. Submitted everything they requested on April 13th, 2020 and received an email confirmation that they would email me if they need anything else.

Then April 16th, 2020 came, and here comes the day of Acid Reflux. The greed of every man for him or herself kicked in, didn't it? We have learned by error to value money over ethics and morals. According to the Oxford Dictionary, greed is described as an intense and selfish desire for something like wealth, power, or food. Could it be that we have allowed greed to create a society that just like Acid Reflux is a result of the overindulgence of wealth, power, or food? What happens when you overindulge in food? You get sick and it can create a serious disease such as GERD.

What happens when you overindulge in power? It can create a series (meaning consecutive occurrence of something) of diseases. What is the definition of disease?

According to Oxford Dictionary, a disease is defined as a disorder of a structure. Don't just take my word for it. Go to the dictionary and look up the word disease. The overindulgence of power is the ability to have influences on others. Now, what happens when you overindulge in wealth? It too, can create a series of diseases. The overindulgence of wealth is to have an abundance of valuable possessions and money.

So, let's walk this back for practicality and application of thought. Why did so many big businesses apply for small business funding? We can point the finger at wealth if you understand what wealth means. Remember, wealth is the abundance of valuable possessions or money. Money can be good. It creates resources and can be used as a means to an end for a result that is necessary and needed. Information can be used just as one would use wealth. Information can be a very valuable possession.

If the haves can access this information, they will literally take it all the way to the bank. However, if the have nots access this same information then they too, can take it all the way to the bank. But because they do not have a history of wealth and information, sometimes they can be left standing outside the bank doors with questions unanswered. To answer the question directly, big businesses applied for small businesses funding because they believed that the valuable possession, they called information, along with insight led them to act on the privileges of their status in wealth. They did not intend on the have nots "having" the wealth information of applying for a small business loan. Historically, the haves bank on the application pool being smaller therefore their scrutiny process did not occur until the 2020 crisis hit.

Question two, why were these large businesses allowed to apply for small business funding and funded immediately? We can now bring power into this discussion. Power is something that can be abusive or helpful. If you have the power to do something, it is up to your discretion to use it as you deem is purposeful to you. Large businesses knew that they did not fit the criteria as a small business, but they applied anyway. They received millions in record timing too. It had to be record timing in order for the entire pot of money to be exhausted in just a matter of days and some hours. Obviously, an abuse of power occurred somewhere.

According to Oxford Dictionary, power is the ability to do something or act in a particular way. You do know that sometimes people in power absolutely love the action of their power. The haves tend to have more experience with power then the have nots. That can seem like an uneven playing field right there in the game of business. One group has insight for resources while another group does not. Large businesses were allowed to apply for small business funding because someone in power had the ability to act in a particular way. The have nots would never have a fair chance at the application process because the atypical have nots, do not have resources or access to resources and power. It is highly unlikely to have both, especially at the same time.

No one intended on the small bakers, AKA (Also Known As) the small businessmen and women, to wave the flag in such great numbers. This flag wave was not a black or white thing so much so, as it was a big business vs small business thing. Black, White, and Brown all complained together when it came down to how the big businesses were treated over the small businesses in which this funding was supposedly earmarked for. All at once power met power, meaning the power of the small bakers rose against the power of the big bakers. This began to hit the news heavy as reports described big businesses returning millions of approved dollars back to the bank.

Early May 2020, we begin to see the news headlines of businesses facing prosecutions for fraud in applying for funding and accepting the loans. While we see the visual crackdown on the news of the business owners that are facing charges for fraud. No one has yet to explain who the power players were, that actually allowed this to happen in the first place. Maybe we don't even need an explanation for this. Maybe that was in someone's power to make the call that explanation was not necessary. The overindulgence in wealth and power can both be just as harmful as the overindulgence in food. Both have similarities and in coordination with disease can show us that the acid reflux of this country is not much different than the acid reflux that can inhibit a human body.

CHAPTER 3

TIME FOR A CHECK-UP

I had a college friend that used to tell me if I knew better, I would do better. Would I? I mean would I really have the inclination to do better just off the premise of knowing better. Sometimes we don't know a lot about ourselves until we get into a position to get to know us. Who had time prior to the pandemic to really take a look in the mirror? Michael Jackson sang the song a man in the mirror. I am asking you to change your ways. A pastor once told me that change comes on the occurrence of obstacles. Whose advice did I like better, the clergy or Mike? It doesn't matter what I think. What matters is what you think at this present time in your life as it relates to check-ups and changes.

What are check-ups? The surgeon general and doctors recommended yearly physicals just as dentists recommend us to schedule yearly oral check-ups. The check-up tells you what is to come, how to prevent it and the changes that are required to treat what the check-up discovered. There you have it, check-ups and changes. The check-up is real out here. It requires self-evaluation and honesty on your part. Learning to be totally honest with yourself can be the most vulnerable conversation you will ever have with yourself. An old boss of mine used to refer to things like this as a "coming to Jesus" moment.

When I worked my first executive position over 25 years ago, my mentorship as a CEO came from this lady. She was stern, she was direct, she was vocal, and hell, she was a lawyer. She welcomed risks as a CEO with open arms. I learned how to lose, and I learned how to win under her leadership. I did not realize until recently that everyone doesn't know how to lose. A few months ago, I was asked to be a guest on a radio show about training people to become successful entrepreneurs. One of the interview questions on that day was advice that I would give to the early entrepreneur. I said the thing that has helped me over the years in being an entrepreneur for the last 25 years is knowing how to lose. I mean you lose, and some people lose with no lesson learned.

One of the things that I learned how to do is lose gracefully. See, I had to learn how to lose so I could learn how to win. You give me a business professional that always wins, and I will show you someone who will have a challenge in recovering from business failures because they have not had enough experience in losing. Losing is an art baby! And when you learn how to lose gracefully you are learning how to take those losses and turn them into wins. You should be able to share those losses with others, so they can recognize what a loss looks like.

Seeing someone else lose can allow you to experience their lessons without being exposed to the loss. If you have not learned anything from your losses, chances are you did not receive a proper loss. Losses build you up to win in your businesses further down the road because you have developed a tougher skin to the things that you are afraid of losing, as it relates to your business. This lesson about losses was learned under the direction of my boss. As the CEO, I saw her get "dragged" and humiliated publicly at meetings, newspaper articles, and social events. Plus, I saw her lose a great deal in business with grant funding and contracts. As she lost, I learned how to win. I also learned how to develop strategies and figure out various ways to bring the company back; soon we were back on top and winning again.

I thought that was the lesson I needed. Learning how to clean up someone else's mess in business. Apparently, there were more things I needed to learn from that experience working under her. What more could I have learned? Well, the only thing I needed to learn in addition to my CEO armor was how to get a check-up. That's right, a personal check-up. I needed to learn my own strengths and areas of improvement that would allow me to also become stern, direct, and vocal. Those are the characteristics that I saw in all lawyers. Hell, I though I would be a lawyer one day too, needing those same characteristics. But these days as a pro-se, I exhibit a lot of those characteristics and some other characteristics that all professionals need; candor, passion, kindness and discernment. You often can become what you admire even if you do not acknowledge it or want it. I never thought about just being myself back then. I only had an image of what I saw others be.

Finding yourself can be quite the chore, especially when your learning curve is shortened by the environment you are existing in. For example, right now, you may be struggling with who you want to be in this economy. Do you want to be employed by others or self-employed? If you choose to be employed by others, chances are you may be at risk for contracting the virus if you work in a place that requires you to interact with the public. If you choose to be self-employed, then you may have the option of creating income from the comfort of your safe home. The biggest question to sort out right now may be to determine, who do you want to be in this economy? What are the parameters of the economy? What does economy mean? Well here goes my acknowledgment of the dictionary.

By the way, I believe that consistent review of the dictionary and its words can enhance your ability to engage thought processes. As a whole, in my experiences prior to the internet age, we had large collections of dictionaries on our desks. My fellow grant writers can most likely attest to this, and the great need we have for this type of support while writing. Reading the breakdown of certain words and languages is necessary for the advancement of communication as my good friend who studies linguistics would say. So, let's do it! Let's start by looking at the word "economy".

According to Oxford Dictionary, the word economy refers to the wealth and resources of a country or region especially in terms of the production and consumption of goods and services. When you look at the status of the economy in May 2020 things look uncertain and unstable. It seems that the world we live in is in TBD mode. To be determined - is on the minds of everyone that has a TV or internet access. What I mean is, that you have to be under a rock with gravel over it to not know what's going on during this 2020 pandemic. This entire experience feels like when you make a sales transaction at a store, then log into your online bank app and it says that the charges are still pending. You log in a week later and the charges are still pending, more stress, more frustration, just waiting for money to leave your account.

Our economy looks like it is still pending. There is nothing more frustrating than waiting on a pending sales transaction to change into a debit from your account. The debit means the transaction is accepted and the money is "off the books." That's something, after that transaction clears, that, I do not have to worry about once the vendor is paid. There is freedom in paying your debts when goods are received. A true example of consideration (money) in exchange for goods or services. But we can't experience that feeling of exchange and transaction cleared at this point with this virus situation. The hardest part of it all is not even having a solid date for things returning back to normal. Sure, they are having discussions of opening up the states and getting us back on track.

The discussion that is difficult to have is the difference between wanting to return back to normal vs. being safe to turn back to normal. If we are putting safety first in our personal check-ups, the challenge is determining what the new normal looks like for you. You will be reviewing what is safe for you and your family in your personal check-up. The psychological impact that this quarantine has caused many individuals cannot truly be documented yet. For some who have never experienced being locked up or isolated for a long period of time, this is mental torture. Then there are the ones who have spent months or years locked up in a prison that totally remember what the experience is like.

The PTSD (Post Traumatic Stress Disorder) experience of this quarantine can trigger other behaviors such as signs of depression, anxiety, hopelessness etc. In fact, whether you have been incarcerated or not, being in this pandemic may be causing you to experience some emotions that are new or have come to the surface. The psychological check-up allows you to check-in with yourself to determine if you need some additional emotional support through this. Many of us do and will need some support before all of this is over and that is okay. I want you to know that it is okay to reach out for support and help. Sometimes a good friend can keep you company. Prayer helps for some. Reading and getting some exercise can increase your endorphins and decrease your symptoms of the "blues." Then there are times when you will need to seek out a mental health professional.

All of this is part of the check-up period and changes we discussed earlier in this chapter. Remember, the check-up period tells you what's to come and how to prevent it. The change period comes once the treatment initiates for what the check-up period discovered. Once you get through the check-up period, it gives you a chance to move towards the changing. Change has a lot to do with the self-evaluation process you have gone through. While you are self-evaluating and making slight adjustments, you create and/or enhance your values.

What you value becomes your economy. Your personal psychological and physical health make the decisions on what the economics of your life and personal space are. Economics speaks to the production, distribution, and consumption of goods and services. When it comes to your personal economy, you control what works for you. How do you stomach this economy? You do so by managing your own personal economy. Your personal economy is what you value in your personal environment. You are in control of your spending habits. You are in control of the information that you allow in your mental space. You control who has access to you in your social space (this is being done with the help of social distancing). You control how much money you save. You control what is a necessary purchase.

You can stomach this economy by using the current circumstances to advance your position. You control what you eat. You have control over how often you eat. You just cannot always control where you eat now. You stomach this economy by taking care of yourself better than you ever have. Do not overindulge in eating. Do not overindulge in spending. Do not overindulge in the behaviors that feed THEIR economy. You must look at nurturing your own personal economy but first, you must self-evaluate so you can find your personal economy.

Once you find it, there needs to be a time frame for you to explore it and nurture that. In psychology, we often say we can't control what others do; however, we can control how we respond. Sometimes no response is better than a response. My Aunt Sallie would tell us when it was storming to sit still and meditate. I would do it and find things within that made me stronger when the storm was over. Just because the world is in a panic and can't find employment doesn't mean that will always be your situation. Maybe employment is not the answer. Maybe starting that business, you always wanted to start is the answer. Do a check-up on yourself and find out what is in YOU during this pandemic that would improve your personal economy. Remember you are in control and dammit, you for sure, are in charge. Build your personal economy, whatever that may look like for you and get through this day by day. Only YOU can do it like YOU do it.

Chapter 4

Dr.'s Orders

Do you have Acid Reflux? I think we all do. You can't resist a perfect buffet of the American Dream that we get sold on. Missing all of that would just not make sense. What we know about acid reflux is simple, it's painful as hell. It's preventable and can be treated once it has been diagnosed by a medical professional. Don't go self-prescribing and problem-solving. You must follow doctors' orders. Following orders, in general, takes great discipline and structure. It's not always easy to become disciplined, especially if you don't already have some form of experience with it.

Discipline starts early, well at least I think it should. I remember when my brother decided to go to the military after high school graduation. A great part of that decision was invoked by my mother's request for him to go. See, in my household growing up, it was always known that we were either going to the military or someone's college. Those were the options because my parents feared that the streets of Saginaw, Michigan would be far more dangerous as the years would come.

They wanted us to make plans beyond where we grew up and where they grew up. My parents were both born in Georgia so they knew the struggle of escaping into a future that would yield more results if they continued to keep their hands on us and keep us disciplined. So, when my brother finished school he went straight to the Navy. My brother referred to the military as a mental strong game. What he meant by that was only the mentally strong were able to withstand the discipline of basic training in the form of yelling, screaming, being cursed out with a superior right in your face on a daily basis. They were put through rigorous boot camp obstacle courses in extreme weather and environmental conditions.

During this time, my brother could see other soldiers falling to pieces right before their superiors' eyes. Some crying, some lashing out at their superiors, and some just quitting and requesting to go home. Not one of these choices were available for him. He was disciplined to keep going. At one point I remember him calling home telling my mom that he wasn't catching on with the skill level it takes to learn how to swim. It was mandatory that he passed his swim tests in order to clear basic training requirements.

Well with discipline used as his motivation, he learned the techniques and passed all of his mandatory swimming tests. When asked, how he was able to discipline himself to learn those swimming requirements in such a short time, his answer was monumental. He said that not passing the test for the Navy was going to be a breeze in comparison to the test he would have to take in explaining to my mother why he was sent home. Not passing his swimming test just wasn't an option on his list of things to do. Besides, our father trained us all for the military in his own personal right. My brother and I often joke about the fact that there wasn't anything the military could say to him that my dad had not already said growing up.

When you are conditioned to pushing forward and rooted in discipline by others, doing those things for yourself becomes second nature. We must grasp discipline in order to survive what we are experiencing and what we are going to experience in months to come. I was led to write How to Stomach This Economy because I knew that this would be a much-needed conversation for those of you who are disciplined enough to pick up the book. I am so glad you did. Not because of book sales but because I believe that you needed some relief. Man, I hate Acid Reflux and how it feels. I also hate poverty and how that feels.

Poverty does not look good on anyone and it for damn sure should not be used as a crutch, comfort, or badge of honor. There is nothing honorable about poverty. Poverty is preventable, don't let anyone tell you different. You have a choice to be or not to be. Just like you have a decision to make about being a Have or being a Have not. Being able to stomach this economy is going to require you to pick a side, either you are going to be a have or you are going to be a have not. Don't stand at the crossroads, you can't afford the consequences of just standing there. Be disciplined enough to make better decisions in regard to your relationships, career, professional development, finances, and self-love.

These are all critical to your survival especially now, in Covid-19 America. Self-love is a great way to believe in yourself. When you believe in yourself you do things better for yourself. Do you believe that you can stomach this economy? That's the question you have to ask yourself as you prepare to discover your answer. Maybe you don't know the answer yet and that's okay for right now. However, before this book is over you should be pretty close to answering yes and answering it with control and confidence. Remember I told you earlier that you were in control. Don't give control back to the forces of the virus. The virus does not control your abilities to innovate and create.

Dr.'s Orders are about following a prescription that is designed to help you treat whatever ran your ass into the dr.'s office. Just like what led you to order a copy of this book. You wanted some solutions from an experienced veteran that's not going to walk on eggshells with you about the main hot topic of YOU! It's important that you gather yourself around like-minded people that can share your headspace of getting through this tough time with solutions and suggestions of building. In order to stomach this economy, you're going to have to build. Building can be very exhaustive -- especially when you do not have experience building and do not know where to begin.

My suggestion is you begin with yourself. Draw a line in the sand and pick a side. Make a choice today. Don't kid yourself or talk yourself in or out of your decision. Are you going to work for someone else all your life or do you want to work for yourself? Now I get it, one is much easier than the other one. One is going to require a hell of a lot of discipline. The other one is going to require that you tighten up your resume and dress that part for the interview. One choice is not better than the other. It is just that the one you choose may be the move you are stuck with for a long while, so choose wisely. I really do wish you the best in whatever you choose.

If you are saying entrepreneurship is your drug of choice for treating the acid reflux of greed, Let's Go! Changing your diet heals the wounds of acid reflux just as changing your mindset heals the wound of financial inadequacy. You have to experience financial healing so you can heal and then turn around and help others heal. Once you help heal others, you will begin to see the language breakdown behind how they found themselves financially wounded in the first place.

The language of currency perception for the haves differ, then of the currency perceptions language of those who are the have nots. Currency perceptions are your worldview of how you view money. Your parents and/or guardians' worldviews about money can be passed on to you and you can possibly pass it on to your children. Have you ever considered your currency perception? How do you perceive money or currency? Some people can see money as a way of purchasing things, while others can see it as a way to leverage assets, so in turn, those assets are used to purchase those same things. Both ways give you the title as a consumer. However, the latter way gives you an "extra play" for creating additional type of currency to make the same purchase. That additional type of currency is assets.

Assets can be accumulated in a lot of different ways. Once you have created assets, you have created additional currency. It is information like this that can create currency; create finances for your current and future projects. Information is currency and currency is the value of and a form of consideration (money) for advancement. What is advancement? Come on now, it means it is another way of getting somewhere. Are you going? If that is a yes, come on, I will meet you in the next chapter so we can get to it. Learning how to stomach the economy takes work. I know you can do it. We are in the home stretch and about to take it home. You got this and you are almost ready to write your own book about your experiences and the ride along the journey.

CHAPTER 5

BUILDING AN ARK

In the bible, it says that Noah built an ark. The ark seemed to be representative of a form of protection from the rain. According to Wikipedia, Noah's Ark is the vessel in the Genesis flood narrative through which God spares Noah, his family, and examples of all the world's animals from a world engulfing flood. Theologians have said that Noah received directions and divine inspiration from God to start building for something he had not yet experienced before, the rain. How can you prepare for something in which you have never had any exposure to? Do you even know what to expect? Imagine getting inspired to build something with no prior knowledge or exposure to it? What would it look like? How would you know that it's completed?

The fear of not knowing can be very frightening. You know that feeling you get when you are waiting on a call back after an interview for a job you really need. How about the experience of sitting in the waiting room of a hospital floor waiting for your loved one's nurse or doctor to tell you the status of a life-threatening surgery. That drop you feel in the pit of your belly when someone tells you that your loan is still pending after waiting for weeks and you need that approval. I remember times in my early twenties when I was purchasing my first car and the finance office told me that my credit did not qualify, and I needed a co-signer.

I felt that same roar in my body after I was denied a basic need such as purchasing transportation to get to and from work. I could not understand it when they said I needed a co-signer. I was offered a couple of credit cards on the college campus I attended, and they gave me credit. I even went to the bank where I opened an account and was offered a credit card as well. None of this could make sense of being denied an opportunity to purchase a new car that I needed. That was my ark and I needed it bad. I needed to be able to travel back and forth to work and school so I could start my adult life as the gainfully employed.

It's a good thing that my father had great credit and a great paying job. He co-signed for my first new car. He put his credit on the line to help me build up my credit score by having a positive primary tradeline experience on my credit report. A primary tradeline is when you have a loan that is directly in your name. A form of a primary tradeline could be your home, automobile, or line of credit. What my father did was build his ark for his family in the form of having good credit.

My mom says my dad always had great credit all his life. In fact, she brags that his credit and his reliability in paying bills were much better than hers as my father was well disciplined in his spending. He worked for General Motors' third shift most of my life. As long as I could remember my dad would work long hours, come home and work in his garden. I learned from him that my grandfather, his dad, ran his own business in the early 1900 as an agriculturist in his own right. My father only had a 3rd-grade education, but he was sharp as a nail when it came to the ingenuity needed to build something.

He gained this talent from his father who also had a reputation in the deep south of Buena Vista, Georgia for building and planting a garden. Both men, my father and grandfather, in their life and their death made great commitments to budget, build, plan, and take care of their family. This preparation for the unknown has been passed down from them to me. As I remember the stories, I heard about my grandfather, Papa, as my Aunt Ray calls him, and my father, John, they planned for the best but prepared for the worst.

Here I am a million years later in the same position of building an ark for my family. A few years ago, I just felt the urge to talk to people about improving their credit because they needed to be ready. Anyone that knows me knows that as I established relationships with people, I would often inquire about their credit score. Not to be nosey or to embarrass them.

However, I had some insight in wanting to make some changes and improvement in my personal credit and wanted them to have access to the same opportunities. Some made jokes about my credit conversations and some became serious. The ones that were serious worked on improving their credit and when the time came, they were ready to start a business and apply for business funding.

Talk about a game-changer for those who finally wanted to become entrepreneurs. Not just doing "business on the side," but running a real business with day-to-day operations and business development. After injections of large amounts of business funding approved, many set their sails towards the sea of real estate investing. Now I have seen many arks being built around real estate investing. I am talking about purchasing a property and renovating it to sell it for big profits. How does an extra $30,000 to $50,000 sound in your bank account all at one time? All because you were funded $150,000 for your business.

You used those funds to leverage an investment loan for $90,000. The renovation needed on that home was about $12,000. You only used $9,000 of that $150,000 of funds you have because another funding source allowed you to borrow up to 90% of the house value. After the $9,000 and the $12,000 you were out of a total of $21,000. After the home was renovated it was valued and sold at $135,000. You paid the lender back the $81,000 ($90K - 10% = $81K) owed thus leaving you with a profit of $54,000.

You now have the resources to put this process on rinse and repeat to build a real estate portfolio. Now of course, this is just an example, but it is a good example of the benefits of a well-built ark called great credit. The credit bureaus are Experian, Equifax, and Transunion. There are others but just like the old school car industry from back in that day, we call them the big three just as we called GM, Ford, and Chrysler. I love the concept of how the big three in the automobile game locked the industry. They were like the super friends of automobiles with special powers like advancing credit to their millions of employees.

If you have ever been to Detroit, Michigan, home of the big three, you would know that the people in this city "drive good." To "drive good" is what I would hear the older men say as they would dote over their brand-new Cadillacs and SUV trucks with fancy wheels and fresh wet looking paint jobs on the latest new automobile. The big three knew that in order to maintain the amount of increased sales for their production of automobiles that they were going to need to extend their employees a large amount of credit to purchase these expensive new cars. In the early 80's it was quite the accomplishment to get selected to work at "the plant" as they called it when you were selected to become a factory worker making those beautiful cars.

Those men and women worked extremely hard taking on two work shifts to make extra money. That money was flowing through the car industry and coming right back to them in the form of sales and lending. While this was great for business it was not always great for the employees as they missed family time and often paid the debt of their health because of some of the jobs not being safe to work. Yet, in time, it was helpful in providing for millions of families and at the moment, building up their employee credit history and optimizing their lending exposure.

That's the recipe for building an ark, great credit and great revenue sources. This build-out of that type of ark has been and will be successful in creating the protection needed to withstand the financial rainfalls to come. Building an ark takes time, it takes discipline, and it takes responsibility. I know you can do it and that's why we are discussing it right now. If you haven't noticed by now, you are going to need to build an ark. You are going to need to build protection for you and your family and whatever animals you choose to bring along.

Remember you are in control so don't forget that. Building an ark means that you have to start improving your personal credit. I am going to share an important document with you at the end of this book, that can help you improve your personal credit. This form is called Understanding & Addressing Your Credit Report. This document will soon be made available for you to download and print. Prior to downloading and printing you can also see all three of your credit scores at **www.ShowMeMyCredit.com**.

Now that you have had a chance to see your credit report and study the issues you can develop a plan for improving your credit. Here are some of the steps you can use to do just that. When you look at your credit report, I want you to see just how many inquiries you have on each bureau. The inquiries are the amount of times someone has asked to look at your credit. If you have for example 6 inquiries, you can times that by 2-3 points (6 inquiries X 3 points = 18 points). That could mean 18 points lost on your credit report. The credit report is broken down by 35% - payment history, 30% - amount owed, 15% - length of history, 10% new credit, and 10% types of credit used.

When you look at the rubric breakdown of how your credit score is calculated you will see that payment history and amount owed is combined for 65% of your credit report. Add in length of history and you can add another 15% for a total of 80%. Think about it now, 80% of your credit report scores are impacted by your payment history, amount owed, and length of history. The other 20% of new credit and types of credit is small to a giant. This means that new credit and the type of credit does not have much impact on your credit score. Store cards vs. Authorized users also does not have a big impact on your credit score.

What are Authorized Users? Authorized Users are tradelines that can be added to your credit report. This occurs when someone with a great credit history on a particular tradeline adds you to that tradeline and their low utilization and credit history length is used to boost your credit score. They lend you their credit history on that particular tradeline to place on your credit report. This can really boost your credit score; however, it can backfire if the one who added you as an authorized user stops paying and has a delinquent bill or increase of their utilization on that credit tradeline. If this happens then you inherit that negative credit history too.

Looking at how your credit score is created it gives you an opportunity to self-evaluate and plan. You must know that when you improve your credit scores it puts you in position to borrow, you must also have a plan to pay that money back. Before you purchase anything, I highly recommend you have a solid plan for paying it back. That solid plan should be in the form of a business plan. Write your business plan so you have a clear plan for starting your business and how that business will make revenues from the first day you open your business doors or business email address -- since quarantine from the virus is calling all the shots these days. 80% of your credit score is depending on this plan.

Before you ask to borrow anything from anyone or inquire about business funding processes, you should have already decided your business industry. By the time you have researched that business and its industry, you should have been working to improve your credit scores. Before you apply for any type of funding you should have participated in some personal and professional development. Let me tell you a little bit about personal and professional development. We can refer to it as PPD. When you are building anything worth standing you want to create it with PPD in mind. Where do you get PPD?

Well, my sister over the years has shown me the ways that she allows PPD into her life and what it does for her. When I was a radio personality back in Detroit, my show format allowed me to bring on co-hosts. One of the co-hosts was my sister. She didn't get her spot on my show because she was my sister. Nope, she held that spot because she is a reading machine. Since childhood, she has always read books of all types of genres. This type of reading history has made her an expert in so many industries because of her tenacity to want to learn and grow personally and professionally. This comes in especially handy when it comes to brainstorming back and forth with her on business ideas.

She has made it her business to "have a dog in the fight" while speaking with the new people she meets. What is it to "have a dog in the fight"? Well, I am glad we are talking about it. What it means is to read as much as you can about various social issues abroad and local just in case you need the information. She finds this most helpful when she is in a new social environment of new professional people. She often talks about the people she has engaged in conversations over the years from Lenny Kravitz's drummer to hedge fund managers.

She likes to have some information in common, that makes her more conversational in elite environments. This conversation is usually information she had read about on a daily basis or researched from a previous conversation from another professional encounter. This information they share allows them to have commonality on relevant social and interpersonal conversational topics. All because she has a "dog in the fight".

Imagine meeting Mark Cuban or Oprah Winfrey in a long elevator or business meeting. You better have a three-minute conversation worth having. Three minutes with the right person can change your business life. That doesn't require that you know everything, but at least know enough to be pleasing to the ears with a conversation that makes the three minutes of conversation pleasurable, exciting, and worth hearing more conversation later. Don't embarrass yourself with not knowing anything about what's going on in the world. Try to spend as much time as you can experiencing PPD so you can expand your vocabulary or world view.

When the television media outlets and news stations back in September of 2019 were talking about a quid pro quo, my sister Googled the term so she would not be caught off guard if a business professional engaged her in small talk about current affairs and topics. PPD is really about taking the time to learn something new that will enrich your experience with others especially the professional people around you.

There are so many opportunities to enrich yourself without spending a lot of money. For example, you can watch PPD subjects on YouTube or check out some Ted Talks. Google has content to research new authors and business professionals, social media outlets and the list goes on.

Ask your network about good books they are reading. Go to your social media and ask your online networks for PPD topics to enhance your personal growth. Self-help books online and blogs can be a great resource for you in that area as well. Do more than you are currently doing so that you too, can have "a dog in the fight". Remember information is the new currency and you have to learn where to find it and when to use it to unlock access. This access to information could be the difference between being a have and a have not.

The PPD process along with some self-evaluation will increase your self-discipline of your actions and spending habits. You have to practice daily in the gym before you can prepare for competition in a race. This is the same for becoming an entrepreneur. Do not jump into the business world unprepared. You have to build an ark with precision and care. Do not just halfway put it up so it can fall down before you can even enjoy the benefits of it and the protection it brings to you and your family. When starting your business and receiving funding, you must have an immediate plan in making the first payment in 30 days.

Having a revenue plan prior to accessing the funding is key because it gives you a strategy for making those first payments. In fact, with great planning and strategies you could have the borrowed funds paid back within 2 to 3 years or less. Like in the example I gave earlier of the person who borrowed $150,000 and used that to leverage a real estate property that made a $54,000 profit. Facilitating three to four more similar deals could have you pay your debts off in a smaller time frame. Now you can guess what that will bring you, right? I hope you said additional capital, because yes, that is the answer!

With the right structure and strategy for your business revenues, you can build a million-dollar or more ark. It just takes that one person that one time to believe. You have to believe in yourself and you have to learn to bet on you. You may be stuck at home waiting on work or at work wishing you can be home working. No matter what the situation is, I want you to be safe, and happy, and successful. Locking down success right now can be a challenge and can look difficult and feel impossible. However, during this time you can do it! We need more Noah's to build an ark.

*"We are not certain about the outcome of this virus, but we can be certain about the end results of our drive for personal change. We can control that. You cannot control how this world's pandemic will impact your finances. However, you can control the information and resources that you have access to during this time of need. Information is the new currency. I hope by reading this book, you are able to enrich your own personal economy and unlock this new currency. Acid Reflux: How to Stomach This Economy, makes the analogy between the medical condition of the human body and the economical condition of humanity. Both are preventable and equally treatable. We have to rely on a community that values information as the new wealth". - **DocTori2.0***

Understanding & Addressing Your Credit Report

www.ShowMeMyCredit.com

Must Have a Copy of All Three Credit Reports for this Exercise

Step 1

Review the summary page of all three credit reports and look for the following information.

Your Name: _____   Date of Credit Report: _____

	TransUnion	Experian	Equifax
Collections			
Delinquent			
Derogatory			

	TransUnion	Experian	Equifax
Credit Score			
Public Records			
Inquiries			

Step 2

List Each **Current Account**: Name / Balance / Limit

1. _____ / _____ / _____
2. _____ / _____ / _____
3. _____ / _____ / _____
4. _____ / _____ / _____
5. _____ / _____ / _____
6. _____ / _____ / _____
7. _____ / _____ / _____
8. _____ / _____ / _____

9. _____/_____/_____

10. _____/_____/_____

Step 3

List Each **Charge-off or Collection Account**: Name / Acct # / Balance / Date Opened

1. _____/_____/_____

2. _____/_____/_____

3. _____/_____/_____

4. _____/_____/_____

5. _____/_____/_____

6. _____/_____/_____

7. _____/_____/_____

8. _____/_____/_____

9. _____/_____/_____

10. _____/_____/_____

Step 4

List Each **Inquiry**: Name / Bureau / Date of Inquiry

1. _____/_____/_____
2. _____/_____/_____
3. _____/_____/_____
4. _____/_____/_____
5. _____/_____/_____
6. _____/_____/_____
7. _____/_____/_____
8. _____/_____/_____
9. _____/_____/_____
10. _____/_____/_____

Step 5

Review each current account and calculate utilization. Utilization is calculated by taking your Credit Balance and dividing it by your credit limit. This will give you a percentage of credit use. For a higher credit score each tradeline utilization should be 25% or below.

Example calculation: Balance $800 / $1,500 Credit limit = 0.5333 or 53% utilization

Account Name / Balance divided by Credit Limit =

1. _____/ $_____/ $_____ = _____%

2. _____/ $_____/ $_____ = _____%

3. _____/ $_____/ $_____ = _____%

4. _____/ $_____/ $_____ = _____%

5. _____/ $_____/ $_____ = _____%

6. _____/ $_____/ $_____ = _____%

7. _____/ $_____/ $_____ = _____%

8. _____/ $_____/ $_____ = _____%

9. _____/ $_____/ $_____ = _____%

10. _____/ $_____/ $_____ = _____%

Activities to Increase Credit Scores

- *If your utilizations in step 5 are over 25% you MUST pay them down to see a credit score increase. Once you pay them down, recalculate to make sure you paid down enough.*
- *Dispute inquiries on your credit report that are not*

- *attached to current tradelines.*
- *Add $14,000 worth of positive tradelines on your credit report such as these links below:*
  www.myjewelersclub.com www.newcoastdirect.com www.huttonchase.com www.oxpublishing.com and www.self.inc . with a secured credit card.
  Open a CD at a bank and borrow against it to create a tradeline.
- *Dispute all collections and charge offs on your credit report. Collection agencies must validate a debt. According to the Fair Credit Reporting Act (FCRA), all items on your credit report must report accurately and true. When you dispute with the credit reporting agencies you are requesting they validate the items on your credit report or remove them in a certain amount of days.*

These are some steps you can do to improve your personal credit scores. Keep your credit monitoring services at Identity IQ active. This will help you stay updated on your credit dispute results. Print multiple copies of this form and reuse after each credit report refresh. These can be used to keep up with your credit report improvements each month.

Go online and Google Credit Report Dispute template and find an example to use. Use one that will use the FCRA as a reference for disputing your derogatory collection information. You have a right to dispute collection and charge offs because your original lender sold it to a third part debt collector. The third party debt collector must be able to produce a signed contract between you and them. If they do not produce this information they must be treated like a stranger trying to steal from you.

If you are 30, 60, or 90 days late on a debt such as a car loan. Try to make at least 90 – 120 positive paid and on time payments before you contact your lender and ask them for a courtesy update to remove past missed payments. If they deny then you can dispute the information and dates of missed payments on your credit report. Remember it's their responsibility to respond in time to your request to update your credit report for accuracy or remove the derogatory information.

ACKNOWLEDGEMENTS

I would like to acknowledge all the front line workers that put their life on the line to save others. I wrote this during the quarantine time of the stay at home order. While at home my family was going through so much as we lost two love ones. I want to acknowledge the loss of my cousin Bobby Ray Oglesby who through my life made me laugh and showed me that I mattered. I will never forget his laughter, corny jokes, and always making me feel like I was a priority all of my life. Thank you! I want to also acknowledge the loss of my cousin Essie Lee Lane. You were always a source of encouragement and love. You spoke your mind and you spoke it well and I have always admired you for that. Thank you for every congratulation and words of motivation after every degree I have.

I also would like to acknowledge my sister Kimberly B Williams for always entertaining my business ideas and new ventures as I scale the walls to find resources to help others in their finances and purpose. Thank you for taking on my last minute requests and letting me be the little sister. I would like to acknowledge my brother Marcus Thomas Brown the middle child of the big 3. You don't ever have to say much for me to know that your proud of me and support me. For all the times I stole your big shoes as a kid and even now if opportunity presents itself. You would see your shoes on my feet or in my closet but you never said a word. Thank you for all of that. When I miss our dad I often look at your pictures to find him in you and there he is.

I would like to acknowledge my support team and friend Carol Johnson. Thank you for helping me with last minute requests and so much more. I appreciate you for all the prayers, listening ear, willingness to be there. God continues to bless me with people like you and my brother Corves Wright. I don't have all the words to describe the brother that I have in this guy. All I can say is what we both say to each other when we get in the trenches. "Loyal to My Loyalty" is all that we will ever say. But right now I will acknowledge and say Thank you!

Special acknowledgement to my cousin Jah'tia Haynes for always stepping in on every project. She has been team DocTori2.0 from day one and I love you from the bottom of my heart. You always make sure I shine like new money in these marketing streets. Thank you! I would also like to acknowledge my manger and friend Marcus Glenn of Mdot Marketing in Augusta Georgia. My granny Maggie Hill passed in 4th quarter of 2019 and she knew I needed an angel. Thank you for your daily inspiration, motivation, and push to greatness.

Final acknowledgment goes to my publisher, mom-manager, business partner, covering, support, and mother Juanita Brown. Thank you for pushing me and not letting me give up. I thank God for you in so many ways. Last but never least, just the greatest, I acknowledge and thank God for teaching me the levels to this game. Prayers work so many miracles as God hears my cry. I'm thankful for every opportunity that He gives me to glorify Him. Thank you Lord for my gifts and your love.

Yours Truly,

Dr. Tori Brown

AUTHOR

Dr. Tori Brown is an experienced business veteran with over 25 years of service, helping new and existing entrepreneurs find their market niche in various businesses. Current works other than business development include real estate investor, music producer, app developer, filmmaker, advocate for underserved populations, researcher, and keynote speaker. In the middle of the Safe at Home Order and quarantine, Dr. Brown knew that it was important to create free resources that would help the American people deal with the financial devastation to come. **The Personal Bailout Plan** can be viewed at no cost to those who register at www.personalbailoutplan.com.

www.ingramcontent.com/pod-product-compliance
Lightning Source LLC
Chambersburg PA
CBHW021413290426
44108CB00010B/509